THE GIFT
of HEAVEN

CHARLES F. STANLEY

THOMAS NELSON
Since 1798

Published in Nashville, Tennessee, by Thomas Nelson. Thomas Nelson is a registered trademark of HarperCollins Christian Publishing, Inc.

Cover photo by Charles F. Stanley

Thomas Nelson titles may be purchased in bulk for educational, business, fund-raising, or sales promotional use. For information, please e-mail SpecialMarkets@ThomasNelson.com.

Unless otherwise noted, Scripture quotations are taken from The New American Standard Bible®, Copyright © 1960, 1962, 1963, 1968, 1971, 1972, 1973, 1975, 1977, 1995 by The Lockman Foundation. Used by permission.

Scripture quotations marked ESV are taken from the ESV® Bible (The Holy Bible, English Standard Version®), copyright © 2001 by Crossway, a publishing ministry of Good News Publishers. Used by permission. All rights reserved.

Scripture quotations marked NIV are taken from the Holy Bible, New International Version®, NIV®. Copyright © 1973, 1978, 1984, 2011 by Biblica, Inc.® Used by permission of Zondervan. All rights reserved worldwide. www.zondervan.com. The "NIV" and "New International Version" are trademarks registered in the United States Patent and Trademark Office by Biblica, Inc.®

Scripture quotations marked NKJV are taken from the New King James Version®. Copyright © 1982 by Thomas Nelson. Used by permission. All rights reserved.

Scripture quotations marked NLT are taken from the Holy Bible, New Living Translation, copyright © 1996, 2004, 2007 by Tyndale House Foundation. Used by permission of Tyndale House Publishers, Inc., Carol Stream, Illinois 60188. All rights reserved.

Scripture quotations marked TLB are taken from The Living Bible copyright © 1971 by Tyndale House Foundation. Used by permission of Tyndale House Publishers Inc., Carol Stream, Illinois 60188. All rights reserved.

ISBN-13: 978-0-7180-9680-9

Printed in Malaysia

24 25 26 27 28 SEM 12 11 10 9 8

Contents

1
Heaven Is a Gift

*T*here is an ever-growing interest these days in living a long life. Think about all the emphasis on good health. Television and radio ads focus on how to strengthen and lengthen life. Off the presses come book after book about health. Magazine and Internet articles are filled with ideas about health practices that can prolong life, or at least allow for a higher quality of life. We have an unquenchable interest in living long, which is natural, and living a high quality of life, which is desirable. So we are focused on the quality of our food and on exercise. There is a lot of emphasis on living in the here and now, but it is all earth-bound. It is all concerned with the immediate, present moment. It asks, *How can I live a better quality of life right now? How can I live longer now?* These are certainly natural and normal impulses. Perhaps you want to live longer because you want to prolong a good thing—you may have everything you need here in this life. You may feel at least some sense of satisfaction with what you have, and the things that you're trying to accomplish. But what about life after this one?

You may *feel* at least some sense of satisfaction with what you have and the things that you're trying to *accomplish*. But what about life after this one?

A Gift from God

If somebody asks you, "What is eternal life?" you might say, "Well, it's everlasting life."

"Okay, what's that?"

This is the answer: Eternal life is a gift from God. It isn't something we work for, something we pay for, something we worship for; it is a gift of God from God.

It's written in the gospel of John and repeated in that passage that all of us know so well from Romans: "The wages of sin is death, but the . . . gift of God is eternal life [through] Christ Jesus our Lord" (6:23).

The wages of sin is death, but the . . . *gift* of God is eternal life [through] Christ Jesus our Lord.

Romans 6:23

A Precious Gift

Eternal life is the gift that God has offered to all humankind. Now, how do we get this gift? How do we access it? Think about this for a moment. When you and I were born, we were born to live forever. Unlike God, we have a beginning. But like God, once our life starts, it is not going to have an ending. God is eternal and everlasting, from Alpha to Omega, the beginning and the end. He has no beginning and no ending. Humans do pass away. We know it's going to happen. It can come at any point in life, at any age. It doesn't make any difference when or where it happens. It's a part of life. But the questions to ask before that time comes are these: *Will I be ready to inherit the gift that God has provided for His children? Am I willing to receive it, willing to accept it, willing to take it as a gift from almighty God?*

Be Ready for Eternal Life

It's important to be ready for the ultimate gift of eternal life. We can focus on two main things when it comes to eternal life: one of them is quantity, and one of them is quality. In regard to quantity, eternal life is everlasting. It has no ending. It cannot be stopped. It is ceaseless: you can't slow it down, can't speed it up. As far as the quality of eternal life is concerned, it is a relationship with God through His Son, Jesus Christ. It is a fellowship, and it is a companionship. There is intimacy in our relationship with Him.

Eternal life is a gift, and it is a relationship.

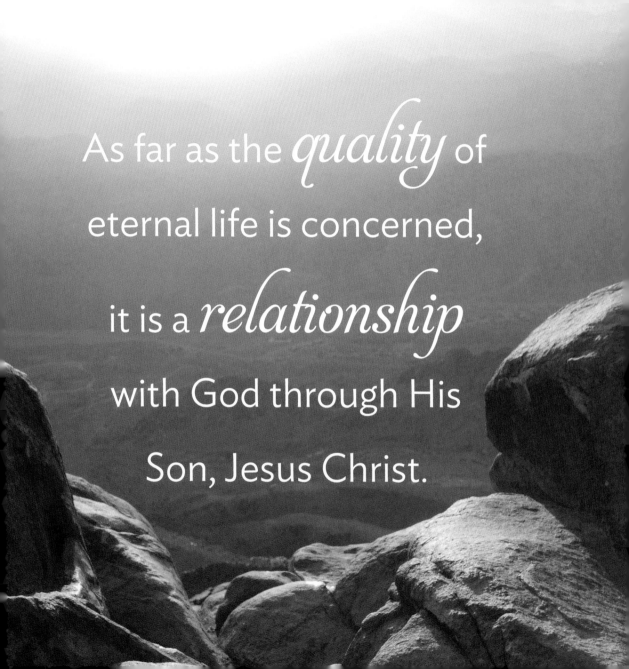

As far as the *quality* of eternal life is concerned, it is a *relationship* with God through His Son, Jesus Christ.

Promises of Eternal Life

"For God so loved the world that he gave his one and only Son, that
whoever believes in him shall not perish but have eternal life."
John 3:16 NIV

For those who find [wisdom] find life and
receive favor from the LORD.
Proverbs 8:35 NIV

"Now this is eternal life: that they know you, the only
true God, and Jesus Christ whom you have sent."
John 17:3 NIV

They will see His face, and His name will be on their foreheads.
And there will no longer be any night . . . They will not have need
of the light of a lamp nor the light of the sun, because the Lord
God will illumine them; and they will reign forever and ever.
Revelation 22:4–5

2

Jesus' Wonderful Promise

When you and I face hardship, sometimes it feels as if it's never going to end. Well, the one thing that's for sure is that it is going to end. There's no such thing as endless trouble. There's no such thing as endless despair for a believer, because every single one of us who is a believer has an awesome promise that Jesus gave on the night before He was crucified.

When Jesus was in the upper room with His disciples, He said to them:

Do not let your heart be troubled; believe in God, believe also in Me. In My Father's house are many dwelling places; if it were not so, I would have told you; for I go to prepare a place for you. (John 14:1–2)

"Do not let your *heart* be troubled."

John 14:1

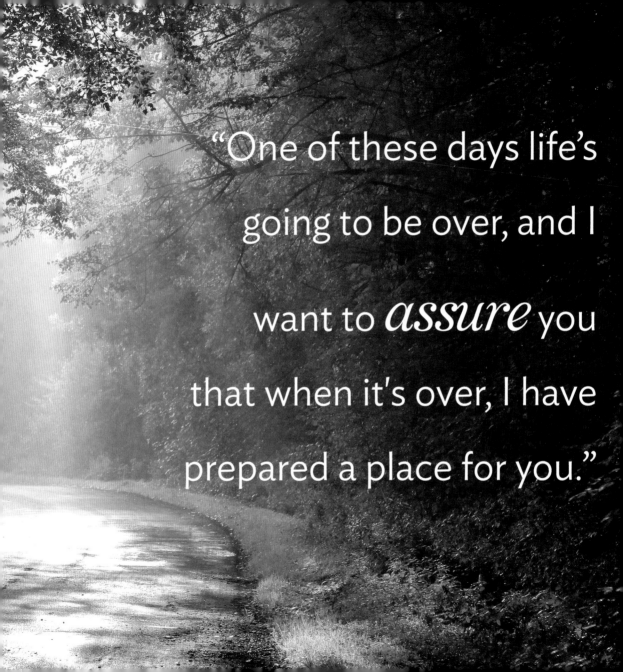

"One of these days life's going to be over, and I want to *assure* you that when it's over, I have prepared a place for you."

Jesus makes a very specific promise about heaven here. He reveals Himself to us and saves us. He works in our life moment by moment, day by day; conforms us to His likeness; builds a relationship with us; comforts us in our hurts; and empowers us. He says, "One of these days life's going to be over, and I want to assure you that when it's over, I have prepared a place for you."

So it's very definite, according to the Scriptures, that heaven is a place that the Lord Jesus Christ has provided and is preparing for all of us who are His children.

Jesus began by saying, "Stop being troubled in your heart." These are words of comfort; remember: the disciples were troubled in this moment. They were feeling despair and unease. What caused them such perplexity?

Back to the upper room. Jesus was washing the disciples' feet. Then, in the middle of washing their feet, "He became troubled in spirit, and testified, and said, 'Truly, truly, I say to you, that one of you will betray Me'" (John 13:21). Now imagine sitting there with Jesus, and all of a sudden, He says, "One of you shall betray Me," without identifying which one. No wonder they were agitated.

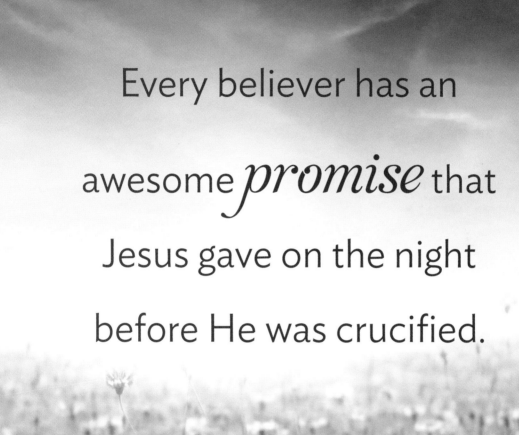

Every believer has an

awesome *promise* that

Jesus gave on the night

before He was crucified.

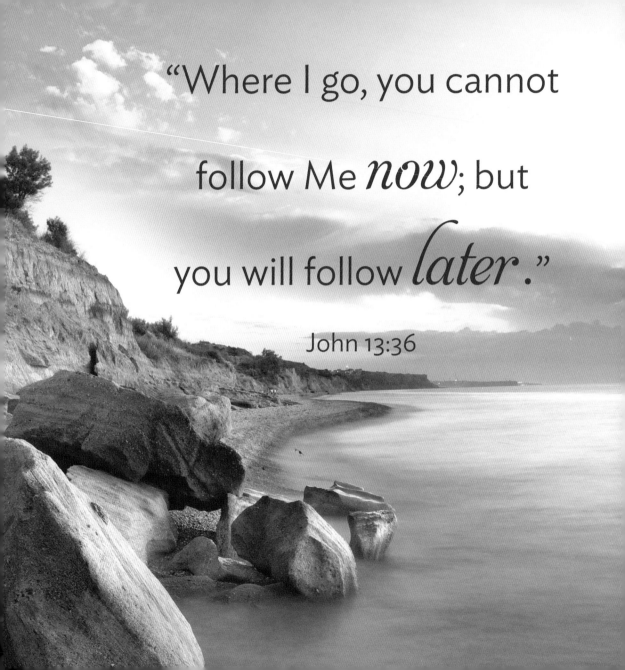

"Where I go, you cannot follow Me *now*; but you will follow *later*."

John 13:36

Jesus continued, "Little children, I am with you a little while longer. You will seek Me; and as I said to the Jews, now I also say to you, 'Where I am going, you cannot come'" (v. 33).

Peter said to Him, "Lord, where are You going?" Jesus answered, "Where I go, you cannot follow Me now; but you will follow later" (vv. 33, 36).

So imagine the kind of distress in their hearts at this moment.

Here's the Lord Jesus Christ, with whom they have walked for three years. They've done what He said to do, followed Him where He said to go. Now He says to them, "One of you is going to betray Me." And to make it worse, He says, "Now, where I'm going you can't follow Me. I'm going to leave you. I'm not going to be with you very much longer, and where I'm going you won't be able to follow Me."

All of a sudden there's frustration, anxiety, wonderment, and uneasiness. "What do You mean, where You're going we can't come? We've been faithful to You. We've followed You. You said You were the Messiah. You are God. You can't take us where You're going?"

All *trouble*

will end one day.

If you're a *child* of God, you are going to *heaven*.

Jesus' Words of Comfort

Then Jesus made this wonderful promise of preparing a heaven for the disciples and for us. He said it as a word of comfort: essentially, "Don't allow your heart to be troubled in the midst of turmoil, strife, disappointment, and despair in life, because it's not going to last forever. You believe in God; believe also in Me." That is always the right response to difficulty, hardship, and despair. That is the right answer to doubts and questions and fears. The right reaction is always to focus upon the Lord and to trust Him.

All trouble will end one day. All suffering, all hardship, all heartache—no matter what it is, it will end. Nothing is forever except God and that which He has promised us.

Now let's think about what Jesus is preparing for us. For two thousand years He has been working on it. Remember: He was a carpenter. It is no accident that Jesus was a builder. I'm sure He's the one overseeing the creation. He's the one working on the holy city called the New Jerusalem—a place that, as the Scripture implies, is the heavenly city (Revelation 21:2). Of this place He says, "Listen. Your citizenship will be inscribed. Your name will be written there. You will be a child of God forever and ever and ever. You can mark it down, set it down, live by it, die by it. If you're a child of God, you are going to heaven."

This is hard to imagine for us. We think in earthly ways even though we attempt to think spiritually in our relationship to God. We have limitations of thought, of abilities, and of capacities. How could there possibly be such a place? We are talking about a heavenly city our Father has provided for us, and there will be enough room for every single child of God: all the way back from Adam to the last person who enters the kingdom of God. There's going to be plenty of room for everybody. And He says He has prepared it for all of us. What an amazing blessing. What an incredible and caring God.

Promises of Belonging

For none of us lives to himself, and no one dies to himself.
For if we live, we live to the Lord; and if we die, we die
to the Lord. Therefore whether we live or die, we are the
Lord's. For to this end Christ died and lived again, that
He might be Lord of both the dead and the living.

Romans 14:7–9 NKJV

But you are a chosen race, a royal priesthood, a holy nation, a people
for God's own possession, so that you may proclaim the excellencies
of Him who has called you out of darkness into His marvelous light.

1 Peter 2:9

But let all who take refuge in you rejoice; let them ever
sing for joy, and spread your protection over them,
that those who love your name may exult in you.

Psalm 5:11 ESV

3

A Glimpse of Heaven

*I*f I asked why you want to go to heaven, what would you say? You might say you want to go there because you think that it is a wonderful place to spend eternity. Perhaps you want to go because you have some loved ones who are already there, and you want to be with them. Or you might want to go because Jesus is there. That's the reason I want to go. We know it will be something greater, far more satisfying, far more fulfilling than earth for the simple reason that nothing in heaven is going to be less than what God has provided here on earth.

Although we rejoice in the idea of heaven, no one alive is qualified to talk about what heaven is going to be like in all its glory. Even though there is much revealed by God, there is much that is unrevealed. All we have is a little sketch of what heaven is going to be like.

Let us take a glimpse of heaven as God has given it to us in His Word. The Bible talks about three heavens.

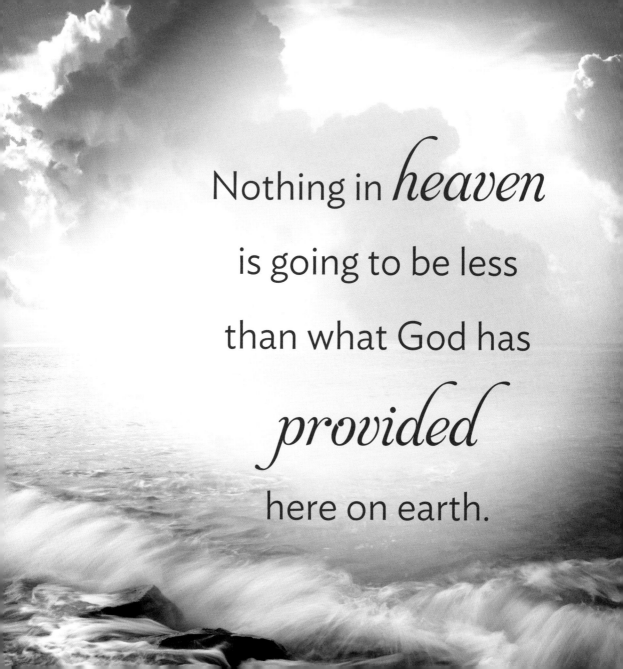

Nothing in *heaven* is going to be less than what God has *provided* here on earth.

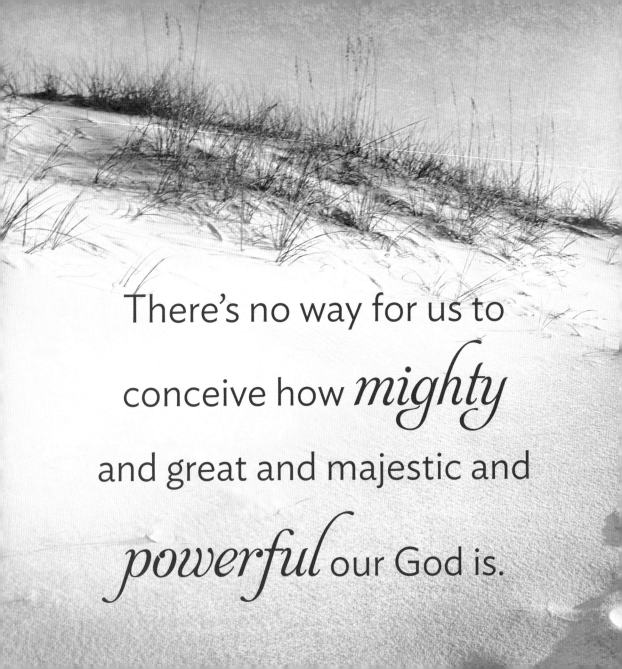

There's no way for us to conceive how *mighty* and great and majestic and *powerful* our God is.

The Three Heavens

First, there's the heaven that surrounds this earth, where we get our rain, moisture, and frost. This contains the clouds, snow, hail, and sleet. It contains the tornadoes and hurricanes, everything in the atmosphere around the earth that inspires awe and grace in all of us. That's heaven number one.

The second heaven is out there in the stellar heavens, where all the galaxies and constellations are. There are billions and billions and billions of stars out there, millions and millions and millions of light-years away. There's no way for us to conceive how mighty and great and majestic and powerful our God is. There's no way the human mind can absolutely contain the greatness of God.

Think of this earth you and I live on—all the beauty, the color, the detail, and the different creatures are things that God has made. Where did it begin? It began in the mind of almighty God. Now, if God can create this earth in six days as He said, can you imagine what heaven is going to be like?

God wants to give us a glimpse.

Paul talked about how God had given him visions, sights so precious that he could hardly speak about them. He said, for example: "I know a man in Christ who . . . was caught up to the third heaven . . . and heard inexpressible words, which a man is not permitted to speak" (2 Corinthians 12:2–4).

Jesus said that *heaven* is not

a figment of the imagination,

a fantasy, or a dream.

John said the holy city

is going to look like the

beauty of a bride dressed

in her finest and looking

her best for her husband.

The third heaven is where God is.

Nobody knows the geographical location of heaven. But let's just say that it is beyond all the galaxies and universes that we know of. Jesus said that heaven is not a figment of the imagination, a fantasy, or a dream.

Everything New

Notice the words John used: "I saw a new heaven and a new earth; for the first heaven and the first earth passed away . . . There is no longer any sea. And I saw the holy city, new Jerusalem, coming down" (Revelation 21:1–2). God is going to renovate this earth. It is going to be absolutely brand-new.

John said there are going to be three new things: a new heaven, a new earth, and a new Jerusalem. When we think of the new heaven, we think in terms of this renovated earth. We liken it to the garden of Eden, in all of its absolute perfection. But that is only part of it.

God described the outside of this new city through John. Now remember this: John was seeing the revelation that Jesus was giving him. As he looked, he saw the holy city, new Jerusalem, coming down, descending toward the earth.

And he said it was the most beautiful thing he had ever seen.

What Does Heaven Look Like?

John said the holy city is going to look like the beauty of a bride dressed in her finest and looking her best for her husband. Then, he said:

And he . . . showed me the holy city, Jerusalem, coming down out of heaven from God, having the glory of God. Her brilliance was like a very costly stone, as a stone of crystal-clear jasper. (Revelation 21:10–11)

If you looked in a dictionary, it would say that jasper is probably a brownish color, yellowish or reddish. But I believe the indication here is that jasper is crystal-clear, more like a diamond. Imagine John seeing this great holy city coming down from God out of heaven, and its brilliance is like a glowing diamond. The glory of God projected from this city.

God is going to

renovate this

earth. It is going to be

absolutely brand-new.

John described the city in detail. He said it had a great high wall with twelve gates, and at the gates stood twelve angels. Names were written on each gate, which were the twelve tribes of the sons of Israel. He described three gates on each side: three on the east, three on the west, three on the north, and three on the south. And the wall of the city had twelve foundation stones, and on them were the twelve names of the twelve apostles of the Lamb (Revelation 21:12–14).

Now, that should say something to us about God's beautiful remembrance—that on these gates are all the names of the tribes of the nation of Israel, and that in these foundations are all the names of the apostles. Here is the awesome beauty and power of God. Here is the remembrance of the love of God. Even in the heavenly city, He is remembering the names of those who were so very important in the nation of Israel.

Whether you and I are going to literally walk on streets of gold is not the point. What John saw was a majestic creation of God, and the only way for him to describe it was to use words that reflect opulence and beauty. It was so overwhelming that he described heaven by using images of gold, silver, and jewels, images that to him were the most valuable and stunning of all. Imagine seeing something so lovely, that's the only way you could describe it!

Promises of Heaven's Beauty

And the twelve gates were twelve pearls, each of the gates made
of a single pearl, and the street of the city was pure gold, like
transparent glass. And I saw no temple in the city, for its temple
is the Lord God the Almighty and the Lamb. And the city has no
need of sun or moon to shine on it, for the glory of God gives it
light, and its lamp is the Lamb. By its light will the nations walk,
and the kings of the earth will bring their glory into it, and its
gates will never be shut by day—and there will be no night there.
Revelation 21:21–25 ESV

The wall was made of jasper, and the
city was pure gold, as clear as glass.
Revelation 21:18 NLT

For he was looking forward to the city that has
foundations, whose designer and builder is God.
Hebrews 11:10 ESV

4

What Will Be in Heaven

(and What Will Not)

We are all curious about what we'll see in heaven. What does the Bible tell us about it? What we see is an indication of what the praise and the worship and the honor of God are going to be like.

Scripture says, "I heard a loud voice from the throne." (Revelation 21:3). It also says, "And He who sits on the throne said . . ." (v. 5). This is followed up with, "Then he showed me a river of the water of life, clear as crystal, coming from the throne of God" (22:1). And still later it says, "There will no longer be any curse; and the throne of God and of the Lamb will be in it" (v. 3). So what is going to be at the heart of heaven? The center of all of heaven is going to be the throne of almighty God.

Who are we going to see in heaven? We are going to see Jesus, and we will recognize Him. The disciples recognized Him, and we will recognize Him too. How will we recognize Him? We will have intuitive knowledge. We will know, as the Scripture says, even as we are known (see 1 Corinthians 13:12).

You and I are going to come into heaven, and at the center of all the activity we will see the throne of God. God the Father, and the Lord Jesus Christ, sit upon that throne. Then the scripture talks about the river of the water of life.

The center of all of *heaven* is going to be the throne of almighty God.

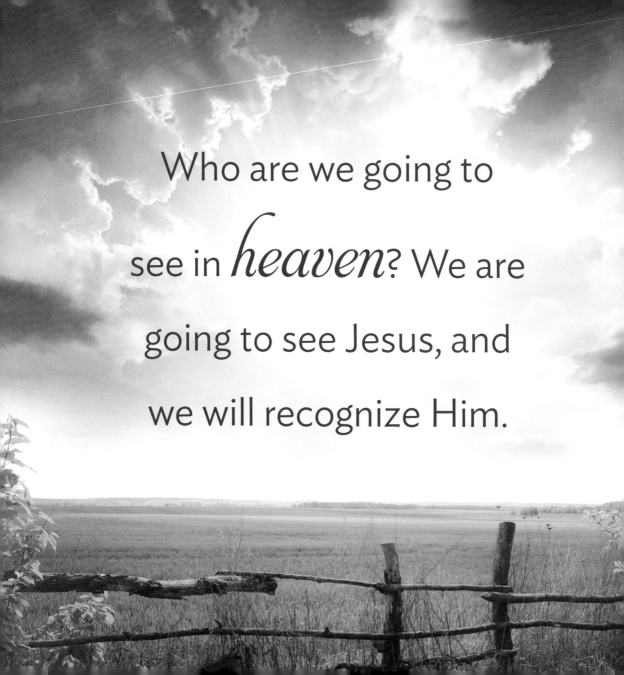

Who are we going to see in *heaven*? We are going to see Jesus, and we will recognize Him.

> Then he showed me a river of the water of life, clear as crystal, coming from the throne of God and of the Lamb, in the middle of its street. On either side of the river was the tree of life, bearing twelve kinds of fruit, yielding its fruit every month; and the leaves of the tree were for the healing of the nations. (Revelation 22:1–2)

That doesn't mean that we have to keep drinking water to stay alive eternally. This passage is really saying that in heaven, there will be an absolute, complete fullness of everything you and I will ever need. The river of the water of life. The tree of life. And when the passage talks about healing, it's not talking about healing from sickness, but rather the absolute, full enjoyment of everything God has created for us in that place.

And so, we see the throne of God. We see the river of life and the tree of life. These are all symbols of everlasting life, of the completeness of heaven. They represent different aspects of our relationships in heaven, the things that are going to be there, and the things that are not going to be there.

There will be an absolute, complete *fullness* of everything you and I will ever need.

The glory of the Lord is going to *brighten* and lighten all of heaven.

What Will Not Be There

What will not be there? In Revelation, John said, "I saw no temple in [the holy city] . . . for the Lord God the Almighty and the Lamb, are its temple" (21:22). So there will not be any church buildings or cathedrals. Do you know why? Because there will not be any Baptists, Methodists, Catholics, or Presbyterians. There will not be any denominations. There will not be any labels, names, or divisions of any kind. We will be the children of God. And we will worship the person of almighty God Himself.

John said there will be no temple in heaven because the Lamb and the Father, the Lord God, are the temple. Likewise, there will be no sun and no moon. When God renovates the heavens and the earth, there will be no need for these elements. This is perfectly explained in this same passage: "And the city has no need for sun or moon, for the glory of God illuminates the city, and the Lamb is its light" (v.23 NLT).

Then John mentions something else that will be missing: "And there will no longer be any night; and [his people] will not have need of the light of a lamp nor the light of the sun, because the Lord God will illumine them; and they will reign forever and ever" (22:5).

"And [God] will wipe away every tear from [our] eyes." When you and I get into *heaven,* "there will no longer be any death."

Revelation 21:4

When we leave these old bodies here, they will be *resurrected* in the absolute perfection of the glorified body of Jesus Christ.

In the Scriptures, *darkness* always alludes to sin. Well, there will be no darkness or shadows in heaven. How is that possible? John said the glory of the Lord is going to brighten and lighten all of heaven. So there will be absolutely no night whatsoever. There will only be His light.

John also said there is not going to be anything unclean in heaven: "Nothing unclean, and no one who practices abomination and lying, shall ever come into it, but only those whose names are written in the Lamb's book of life" (21:27). There's not going to be any sin or immorality. There are not going to be any of the vices or distractions that we turn to here on earth, because we will not have a need for them. He said, "And [God] will wipe away every tear from [our] eyes." When you and I get into heaven, "there will no longer be any death" (21:4).

No Death or Suffering

Now, think about that. There will be no death. There is not going to be any decay or disintegration. Not only is no person going to die, but nothing that God has created in this new heaven will die. For example, if He makes trees, and grass, and flowers—whether it's on this earth or in the holy city—nothing He creates is going to die.

These bodies of ours will be in their glorified form. We will live forever, which is beyond our comprehension in this life. John said in verse 4, "There will no longer be any mourning." There is not going to be any sadness, depression, weeping, disease, blindness, deafness, or paralysis. Everything that hinders this body is going to be gone.

When we leave these bodies, we leave every single *solitary* thing that causes us a problem right here in this life.

When we leave these old bodies here, they will be resurrected in the absolute perfection of the glorified body of Jesus Christ. That's why He says through John that all these things that bear us down—these things that hinder us and cause us heartache and pain and suffering and separation—are going to disappear. None of that's going to be in heaven. We will be walking in the absolute perfection of the joy, the grace, and the love that the Lord Jesus Christ has provided for us.

Because, you see, the grace of God has not only provided salvation here. The grace of God provides heaven, and an existence with no mourning, no crying, and no pain. There are people who live with pain every day. And sometimes they want to die because of it. But when we leave these bodies, we leave every single, solitary thing that causes us a problem right here in this life.

Your Glorified Body

The Bible says that you and I are going to have glorified bodies in heaven. The apostle Paul says our citizenship is in heaven, and we eagerly wait for the Lord Jesus Christ, who will transform these physical bodies of ours into conformity with the glorified body of Jesus by the power that He has to subject all things to Himself (Philippians 3:20–21).

Our bodies are going to be transformed like the body of Christ (1 John 3:2). His glorified body was a material body that was visible and could be touched and could eat fish and drink water. So our bodies are going to be physical bodies because they are going to be in a physical place: heaven.

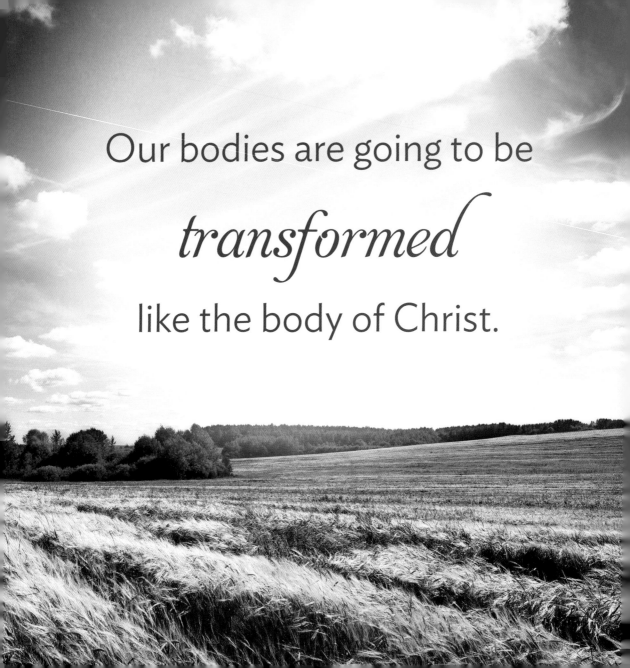

Our bodies are going to be

transformed

like the body of Christ.

Paul spoke a great deal about the body. He said, "It is sown a perishable body"—subject to decay, sickness, and disease—but "it is raised an imperishable body" (1 Corinthians 15:42).

Paul continued, "Just as we have borne the image of the earthy, we will also bear the image of the heavenly" (15:49). This is further proof that our bodies are going to be like the body of the Lord Jesus Christ in heaven.

Furthermore, when you and I come into this relationship of having a glorified body, we are going to be recognizable—much as Jesus was after the resurrection (John 20:16–20) and Moses and

Elijah were during the Transfiguration (Matthew 17:3-4; also 1 Corinthians 13:12). We are going to have the individual characteristics that make us up. We will be recognized. I believe we will have voices similar to the ones we already have. Our personalities are not going to change, except that they're going to be absolutely sanctified. We will be holy, perfect people. We may have struggles down here on earth, but up there we are going to be eternal and glorified versions of ourselves (2 Corinthians 3:17–18). Almighty God will have brought us into our home and His everlasting and perfect love.

These glorified bodies are going to be made for a new environment: the holy city and the renovated earth. They will be absolutely perfect bodies for an absolutely perfect environment.

We may have struggles down here on earth, but up there we are going to be *eternal* and glorified versions of ourselves.

Promises of a Glorified Existence

So is it with the resurrection of the dead. What is sown is perishable; what
is raised is imperishable. It is sown in dishonor; it is raised in glory. It is
sown in weakness; it is raised in power. It is sown a natural body; it is raised
a spiritual body. If there is a natural body, there is also a spiritual body.

1 Corinthians 15:42–44 ESV

For "In him we live and move and have our being"; as even some
of your own poets have said, "For we are indeed his offspring."

Acts 17:28 ESV

Beloved, we are God's children now, and what we will be
has not yet appeared; but we know that when he appears we
shall be like him, because we shall see him as he is.

1 John 3:2 ESV

. . . that the God of our Lord Jesus Christ, the Father of glory, may give
to you a spirit of wisdom and of revelation in the knowledge of him.

Ephesians 1:17

5

In the Presence of God

*I*f you enjoy being with people you love and being in the presence of the Lord God, then you are going to love heaven.

When I think about and read what the Lord Jesus said in the book of Revelation, one thing for sure is that we are going to spend a great amount of time together. We will be spending time with God the Father, the Son, the Holy Spirit. And we will be with each other.

I often reflect on the struggles that I personally face, and the hardships that I have personally gone through as a human being and one of God's children. Sometimes when I am praying, I can't fully express what I feel to God. No matter what I say in my prayer, no matter how much I try to convey my feelings and thoughts, I feel that I am inadequate in expressing how much I love Him. I want to hug the Lord Jesus. I want to feel His presence. I want to bow down and see Him, but I cannot get to Him. Oftentimes I find myself, as Paul said in Romans 8:26, crying out to God and talking to Him, not even knowing exactly how to express what I feel, not making any particular petition or praying for someone else, but just talking to Him. I want an intimate relationship with Him.

If you enjoy being with people you love and being in the *presence* of the Lord God, then you are going to love heaven.

I think He creates within our hearts a desire of intimacy with Him. It is impossible to describe because it is hard to imagine that kind of intimacy as a human being, not yet in a glorified form. Husbands and wives can have intimacy with one another in their thinking and in their conversation and in their physical and spiritual closeness. In our relationship to the Lord Jesus Christ, God also wants us to have an intense intimacy with Him. It is an intimacy that I do not think that we on this earth will ever be able to express adequately. I know I cannot, as much as I may try to tell Him how much I love Him, how much I worship Him, how much I want and need Him in my life, how much I want to walk in absolute obedience to Him. No matter what I say and what I do, there

is something beyond my capacity to be able to express this feeling fully, and to be enveloped in what I know will be a part of our heavenly life. Because two people, no matter how much they may love each other, will never be absolutely able to agree on every single thing. In heaven, there will be a harmony and peaceful coexistence that is beyond our ability to comprehend now.

When you and I get to heaven, there is not going to be any disagreement or any discord. There is not going to be any competition. No one is going to try to control anyone else. There will not be any human agenda. There will not be any gossip, or criticism, or contempt. It is going to be absolutely perfect oneness with others and with God, especially in the person of the Lord Jesus Christ.

In our *relationship*
to the Lord Jesus Christ,
God wants us
to have an intense
intimacy with Him.

Now, this idea that people in heaven are going to float around like angels with wings and rest and relax is not written anywhere in the Bible. The only thing the Bible says with all certainty that we will do in heaven is serve God, and also that we are going to reign with Him.

I believe that the capacities, talents, and gifts God has given us down here will also belong to us in heaven. We will use our gifts and strengths in heaven to worship and praise and serve the Lord Jesus Christ. We will be instruments of His peace. We will be praising Him forever and ever and ever.

God will be able to use us in the most amazing ways, but one thing is for certain: we are going to actively help God in heaven. In the parables Jesus gave, He said, "You were faithful with a few things, I will put you in charge of many things; enter into the joy of your master" (Matthew 25:21).

The more faithful you and I are down here, the more obedient we are, and the more we try to do our best at whatever He calls us to do, the more responsibility He will give us in heaven and the greater the ways we will be able to serve Him in heaven.

In heaven, there will

be a harmony and

peaceful *coexistence*

that is beyond our ability

to comprehend now.

Who Is the Greatest?

Everybody is not going to be doing the same thing in heaven. There is not going to be any insignificant job over here, and a great big significant job over there. All of heaven is going to center around the throne of God. There's not going to be but one star in heaven, and that's almighty God Himself. Jesus is the only One who is going to be onstage in heaven. Humans will not fight for status. All the people on earth who are prominent, all the people with titles and prestige, all the people who have accrued more wealth and have better titles, none of that is going to exist in heaven. When you and I get to heaven, there is going to be One great person seen there above the rest, and that is the person of Jesus Christ. The only thing that will be different for each of us is the way we serve Him.

Your Assignment

We will not just live in heaven forever and ever, but reign forever and ever. God is going to give us places of authority, places to serve Him, places for which we will be responsible. In this life all of us have certain assignments. When you take a job at a business, your superiors give you an assignment, and a certain authority that goes with that. You are responsible, and you have to do that work. One of the reasons people do not always do their best is that they fear failure. In heaven, there will be absolutely no fear. You know what that means? Not a single solitary person in heaven will ever fail at the assignment God gives him or her.

God will be able to use us

in the most *amazing*

ways, but one thing is for

certain: we are going to

actively help God in heaven.

You will be an absolute total success at every single thing He calls you to do. You will not make mistakes. Your language will be perfect. Your attitude will be perfect. Your voice will be perfect. Everything will be perfect.

Not only are we going to have fellowship, not only are we going to serve Him, He says, but we are going to worship Him. Revelation is full of passages that have to do with worshipping God. It says,

"And the four living creatures, each one of them having six wings, are full of eyes around and within; and day and night they do not cease to say, 'HOLY, HOLY, HOLY, IS THE LORD GOD, THE ALMIGHTY, WHO WAS AND WHO IS AND WHO IS TO COME'" (4:8).

All through Revelation, we find God's children worshipping and praising God. Do you know that feeling when everything inside wants to rejoice? Can you imagine millions of angels and all of us singing in tune, knowing all the words? We are going to be singing together to the glory and the honor of God. His majesty and power will be such that everything within our glorified bodies will be able to express itself in perfect worship of Him. We can't even begin to imagine what heaven's going to be like, but we don't want to miss it.

All the *people* on earth who are prominent . . . all the people who have accrued more wealth and have better titles, none of that is going to exist in *heaven*

Not a single solitary person in *heaven* will ever fail at the assignment God gives him or her.

Now, that's a beautiful notion. That is a community we can belong to and an activity that will make us perfectly and absolutely fulfilled. We are God's children. Let us rejoice in Him forever.

We can't even begin to *imagine* what heaven's going to be like, but we don't want to miss it.

Promises of Fellowship and Service

We who had sweet fellowship together
walked in the house of God in the throng.
Psalm 55:14

If we walk in the Light as He Himself is in the Light,
we have fellowship with one another, and the blood
of Jesus His Son cleanses us from all sin.
1 John 1:7

I pray that the fellowship of your faith may become effective through
the knowledge of every good thing which is in you for Christ's sake.
Philemon 1:6

[Speak] to one another in psalms and hymns and spiritual songs,
singing and making melody with your heart to the Lord.
Ephesians 5:19

6

Those You Love in Heaven

There is one question that all children of God have wondered about at one time or another. It's an important and personal question. For some of us, it's the biggest question we have about life after this one. The question is simply this: Who is going to be in heaven?

This is a big question. After all, our lives are filled with people whom we love and cherish. We want to know if we will be able to spend eternity with our families and friends. We want to know who will be beside us in the glory and light of God.

The Lord God and All His Angels

The answer to who is going to be in heaven is in the Bible. First of all, it tells us that God is in heaven. Scripture mentions several times that God is in His throne or on His throne, and the Bible says that "the throne of God and of the Lamb shall be in it, and His bond-servants will serve Him" (Revelation 22:3). So you and I know that God the Father is going to be there, God the Son is going to be there, and God the Holy Spirit is going to be there.

We also know that the Bible speaks of angels all through the book of Revelation, and one thing for certain is that there will be many, many angels in heaven. For example, the Bible says, "I looked, and I heard the voice of many angels around the throne and the living creatures and the elders; and the number of them was myriads of myriads, and thousands of thousands" (Revelation 5:11). It talks about the angels around the throne singing a new song.

I looked, and I heard the voice of many *angels* around the throne and the living creatures and the elders; and the number of them was myriads of myriads, and thousands of thousands.

Revelation 5:11

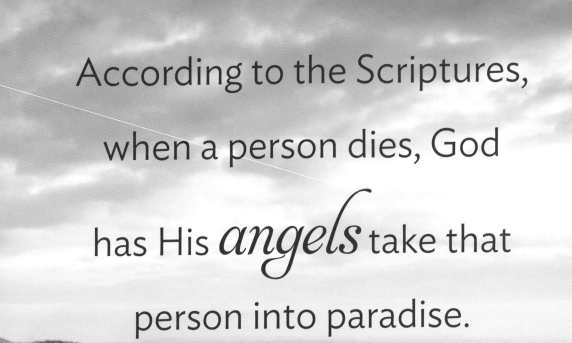

According to the Scriptures,
when a person dies, God
has His *angels* take that
person into paradise.

Remember that God created angels as His messengers to carry out His work. When people ask, "Do you think we have angels looking after us on earth?"—well, that's a matter of opinion. Some people feel that they do, and some people feel that they do not. But one thing is clear according to the Scriptures. The Bible says that when Jesus talked about the rich man and Lazarus, the rich man died and went to torment, and when Lazarus died, the angels carried him into paradise, or Abraham's bosom. So according to the Scriptures, when a person dies, God has His angels take that person into paradise.

Just think about that miracle. Think about being brought up into eternal life by thousands of angels. That is a beautiful image.

Friends and Loved Ones in Heaven

One of the other wonderful things about heaven is that all our friends and all our loved ones who have passed on before—if they died having received the Lord Jesus Christ as their personal Savior—are also going to be in heaven. The scripture says that, when Jesus comes again, He is going to bring with Him those of our loved ones who have passed on before us (1 Thessalonians 4:13–14). So we know friends and loved ones and parents are going to be there.

All of those who placed their faith in God are going to be there. Angels are going to be there. People from all nations will be there.

All of those who placed

their *faith* in God

are going to be there.

Our Relationships in Heaven

Now, when it comes to who is in heaven, the second thing to think about is what kind of relationships we are going to have there. How will we relate and connect to one another? Well, to answer that question, we have to go back to this idea of glorified bodies. You will recall the apostle Paul said that "our citizenship is in heaven, from which also we eagerly wait for a Savior, the Lord Jesus Christ; who will transform the body of our humble state into conformity with the body of His glory, by the exertion of the power that He has even to subject all things to Himself" (Philippians 3:20–21).

Therefore, our bodies are going to be transformed like the body

of Christ—and remember that His glorified body was a visible, physical body. And glorified bodies are imperishable.

A significant passage to think about when it comes to the relationships we will have in heaven with our glorified bodies is where Mary Magdalene and Jesus met in the garden after His death. This is a significant moment, because most of us wonder what we are going to be like in heaven, and how other people will be able to recognize us when we are there. So Mary was standing outside the tomb, weeping. Then the Scripture says, "When she had said this, she turned around, and saw Jesus standing there, and did not know that it was Jesus." Now, she saw Him, but she did not know it was Him. "Jesus said to her, 'Woman, why are you weeping? Whom are you seeking?' Supposing Him to be the gardener, she said to Him,

'Sir, if you have carried Him away, tell me where you have laid Him, and I will take Him away.' Jesus said to her, 'Mary!' She turned and said to Him in Hebrew, 'Rabboni!'" (John 20:14–17).

Notice that she looked at Him, and at first she didn't recognize Him. He had a glorified body, so there was some difference, some change. Remember the last time she saw Him, He was stretched out on a cross and covered with all that bloody ugliness. What was it that made her recognize this was Jesus? It was what He said. It was His voice.

This is a familiar scene for us all in some ways. Oftentimes, I'm somewhere in a crowd, or sometimes I'll be on a plane, and somebody will walk up to me and say, "You know, I didn't recognize you

When you and I have our *glorified* bodies . . . the people who love us are going to know us, and we are going to know them.

until I heard you speak." And then, "I've heard your voice so many times I knew this had to be you." Well, this is exactly what happened to Mary. When she saw Jesus, she wasn't expecting Him, and there was something about Him that was different enough that she didn't quite recognize Him at first. But when He called her name, she knew that voice.

Now, when you and I have our glorified bodies, we are going to be recognizable, and we are going to have similar voices to the ones you and I have now. We are going to be recognized just as we are down here. The people who love us are going to know us, and we are going to know them.

The reason I say this much about the body is because of Jesus Christ. You will recall that Jesus went to the apostles and He walked in and showed them His hands with the nail marks in them. Yet, even while they were looking at His hands, they were having a hard time believing that it was Him. Then He said, "Do you have anything to eat?" And they gave Him a piece of broiled fish, and He ate it, and He digested that fish even though He had a glorified body (Luke 24:36–43). So you and I will never be able to explain humanly what that glorified body is going to be like, except that it is made to perfection for its new environment.

The one thing we know for certain is that the *glorified* body will be absolutely perfect.

People always ask me specific questions about their bodies in heaven, like, "If I die at seventy-five, what am I going to look like?" Well, I can't answer that question. I can tell you this. You are going to be the best-looking seventy-five-year-old you've ever seen. Or I am asked, "Well, suppose a person dies as a baby. Will that person always remain a baby, or will they grow up?" Nobody knows the answer to that, so all those things are conjecture. We just know some things that are absolutely certain, given to us in the Scripture. Anything else is our imagination, and yours is as good as mine.

The one thing we know for certain is that the glorified body will be absolutely perfect. It will be the best that almighty God can do, and we will be perfectly, totally, and completely fulfilled.

Knowing Our Friends and Family

People also often ask if they will only know their families and friends in heaven. The truth is, we are going to know more than what we know now; we are going to recognize all God's children. Let's take a look at Matthew. Jesus has taken Peter, James, and John up on the mount, and this is the account of the Mount of Transfiguration:

> Six days later Jesus took with Him Peter and James and John his brother, and led them up on a high mountain by themselves. And He was transfigured before them; and His face shone like the sun, and His garments became as white as light. And behold, Moses and Elijah

appeared to them, talking with Him. Peter said to Jesus, "Lord, it is good for us to be here; if You wish, I will make three tabernacles here, one for You, and one for Moses, and one for Elijah." (Matthew 17:1–4)

Now, how did they know that was Moses and Elijah? Jesus didn't make an introduction. He didn't identify anyone, so how did they know it? The answer is *intuitive knowledge*. They just knew.

What is intuitive knowledge? Intuitive knowledge is knowledge that you and I have without a conscious action on our part. It is a God-given and innate knowledge. It is a core component of our life in heaven, because it is the element that will enable us to have an intimate, loving, and overwhelmingly and unimaginably close relationship with God. It is the last link in the chain of community in heaven above.

Promises of Community

Let us consider how to stir up one another to love and good works, not
neglecting to meet together, as is the habit of some, but encouraging
one another, and all the more as you see the Day drawing near.
Hebrews 10:24–25 ESV

Bear one another's burdens, and so fulfill the law of Christ.
Galatians 6:2 ESV

"For where two or three are gathered in
my name, there am I among them."
Matthew 18:20 ESV

But you are a chosen race, a royal priesthood, a holy nation, a people
for his own possession, that you may proclaim the excellencies
of him who called you out of darkness into his marvelous light.
Once you were not a people, but now you are God's people; once
you had not received mercy, but now you have received mercy.
1 Peter 2:9–10 ESV

7

Having Ultimate Fulfillment in Heaven

When we get to heaven, we will know one another. It is God's gift to us.

Paul focused on this idea. I am not going to say that everybody is going to know every single person in heaven, but it's worth looking at this passage: "For now we see in a mirror dimly, but then face to face; now I know in part, but then I shall know fully just as I also have been fully known" (1 Corinthians 13:12).

We will know one another. We will understand and recognize one another. We will have the same names. For example, Revelation says, "He who overcomes will thus be clothed in white garments; and I will not erase his name from the book of life, and I will confess his name before My Father and before His angels" (3:5). So, again, I believe not only are we going to have the same faces, but we are also going to have the same names. We will be absolutely recognizable to one another, because this is heaven. This is where

God's great family is going to congregate for all eternity. This is the stopping-off place.

If we spend eternity together, certainly we want to know each other and recognize each other. I think many people who have had their loved ones pass on before want to see them again when they get to heaven. When I get to heaven, I certainly want to see my mother. We all want to see our parents, or sons and daughters, or whomever it may be that we have loved.

Husbands and Wives

On one occasion, the Pharisees and Sadducees brought up an issue of a person who has been married to more than one husband. Jesus said, "In the resurrection they neither marry nor are given in marriage, but are like angels in heaven" (Matthew 22:30).

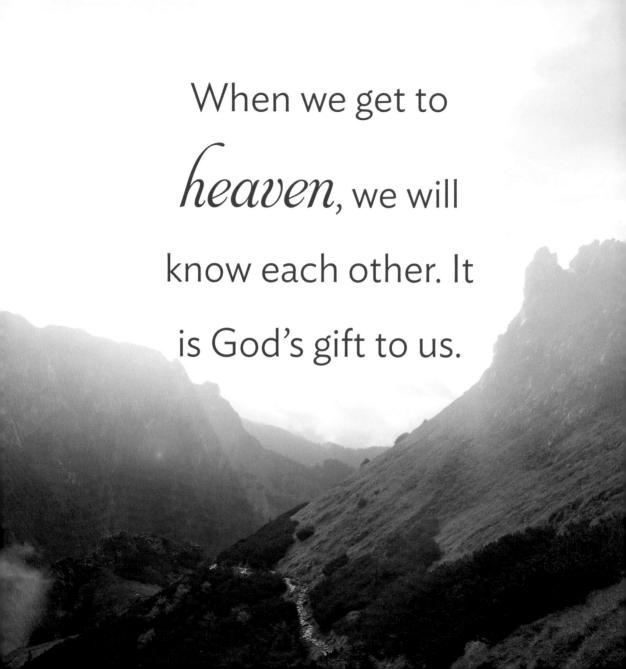

When we get to *heaven*, we will know each other. It is God's gift to us.

Heaven is where God's great family is going to congregate for all eternity.

Now, what did He mean by that? He meant that in heaven, our relationships are going to be such that there will not be a husband-and-wife relationship as we know it in this life. There will not be family as we know it. What is it going to be like? I don't think anybody can answer that specifically except to say this: the relationships we have in heaven will reach a higher form of relationship than even the most intimate of marriages.

Husbands and wives down here love and have an intimate relationship with one another. So perhaps we wonder, *How is it going to be in heaven if I love somebody with all my heart, and when we die I won't ever have that relationship again?* The truth is that relationships in heaven will exceed our capacity to relate to a husband or wife in this life. It will be something greater, far more satisfying, far more fulfilling than earthly relationships for the simple reason that nothing in heaven is going to be less than what God has provided here on earth.

The *relationships* we have in heaven will reach a higher form of relationship than even the most intimate of marriages.

If two people love each other with all their hearts, have a wonderful marriage and relationship, then no matter how great it is, in heaven that relationship will be even greater. That is the power of God. He can create a relationship in a heavenly atmosphere of which you and I can only have a brief glimpse. We do not know the power of God to create those kinds of relationships.

Love for the Father

I cannot fully express to Jesus what I feel. I want an intimate relationship with Him. I think inside, we all do.

I am talking about a hungering, thirsting, yearning desire within us to come into absolute oneness with Him. This oneness is an intimate relationship, and it requires that our hearts be pure before Him and that our desire is to walk in oneness with Him, fully surrendered to Him, fully dependent upon Him, fully trusting in Him, fully focused upon Him, desiring to live obediently before Him so that what satisfies us most of all is that relationship.

He gives us people—friends and husbands and wives and children—to have intimate relationships with and to have fulfillment with, but our ultimate relationship is with Him. I think in all our hearts there ought to be that desire. What He gives us is an insatiable

hungering and thirsting to know Him, to want Him, to walk with Him, and to sense this absolutely indescribable oneness with Him.

If you think about all that you and I know about Him, it is very little compared to what we *could* know about Him. The more intimate we become with Him, the more we understand Him. It's just like a husband and wife. If two people marry, and they just see each other once in a while and never talk or become intimate with each other, they'll never know each other. Intimacy is knowing. God wants us to know Him.

If two people love each other with all their hearts, have a *wonderful* marriage and relationship, then no matter how great it is, in heaven that relationship will be even greater.

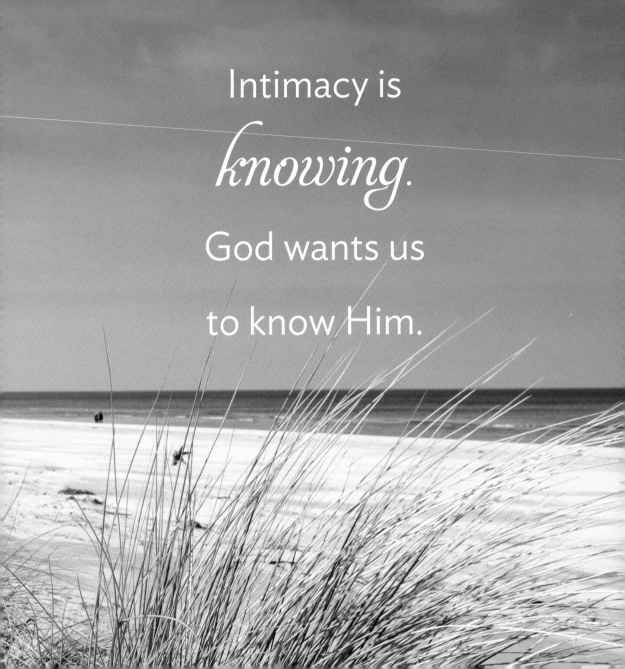

He loves us. He wants us to know Him above everything else in life, because He knows that the more you and I know Him, the more we're going to love Him. The more we love Him, the more obedient we're going to be. The more obedient we are, the more we're going to want to serve Him, and so it's like a domino effect that is at the core of our spiritual existence.

Knowing Him affects every single thing. In heaven, there will be an intimate absolute oneness of perfect fellowship with Him and perfect fellowship with each other.

Promises of Intimacy and Fellowship with God

"Behold, I stand at the door and knock. If anyone hears my voice and opens the door, I will come in to him and eat with him, and he with me."
Revelation 3:20 ESV

"I am the vine; you are the branches. Whoever abides in me and I in him, he it is that bears much fruit, for apart from me you can do nothing."
John 15:5 ESV

"My sheep hear my voice, and I know them, and they follow Me."
John 10:27

Do not be anxious about anything, but in every situation, by prayer and petition, with thanksgiving, present your requests to God. And the peace of God, which transcends all understanding, will guard your hearts and your minds in Christ Jesus.
Phillippians 4:6–7 NIV

8

What Makes the Promise of Heaven Possible?

All this talk about a personal relationship with God and an eternal oneness with God brings us to the only way to reach God: through the Lord Jesus Christ, the Savior.

To believe in Jesus means that I have a confident conviction that Jesus is who He says He is. And upon placing my trust in Him as my Savior, I enter into a personal and eternal relationship with Him. I believe in what He did at Calvary on my behalf. It is my faith that cements my relationship to God as one of His loyal and loving children. It is my faith that makes the promise of heaven possible for me and for all those who believe.

It is my *faith* that makes the promise of heaven *possible* for me and for all those who believe.

There is only one

door into *heaven*.

And the question is,

have you ever

entered that door?

The Narrow Gate

To understand the importance of the role that Jesus plays in eternal salvation, let's turn to Matthew: "Enter through the narrow gate; for the gate is wide and the way is broad that leads to destruction, and there are many who enter through it. For the gate is small and the way is narrow that leads to life, and there are few who find it" (7:13–14).

Did you hear that? There is only one door into heaven. And the question is, have you ever entered that door? There are no side doors. There are no back doors. There are no trap doors on the bottom, and there are none on the top.

You might think that approach is narrow-minded, but the God who created heaven is the One who said there is only one door. In fact, Jesus said it. He said, "I am the door" (John 10:7, 9). He also said, "I am the way, the truth and the life; no one comes to the Father but through me" (John 14:6).

My friend, the question is, what is the truth? Not, what do you and I feel? Not, what do we think? Not, what is our idea about life? But, what is the truth that God teaches in His Word?

One night, a leading religious man named Nicodemus secretly

went to see Jesus. Nicodemus was a leader, a ruler of the Jews, and a teacher. Nicodemus said to Him, "Rabbi, we know that You have come from God as a teacher; for no one can do these signs that You do unless God is with him" (John 3:2).

When he said, "we know that," that means that Nicodemus, no doubt, had been talking to some of the other Pharisees, and they had concluded, "This is no ordinary rabbi. There's something different about this man. And the miracles He's performing cannot be explained in human terms."

The New Birth

So, when Nicodemus said to Jesus that He must be from God, immediately Jesus responded to Nicodemus by saying:

"Truly, truly, I say to you, unless one is born again he cannot see the kingdom of God." Nicodemus said to Him, "How can a man be born when he is old? He cannot enter a second time into his mother's womb and be born, can he?" Jesus answered, 'Truly, truly, I say to you, unless one is born of water and the Spirit, he cannot enter into the kingdom of God. That which is born of the flesh is flesh, that which is born of the Spirit is spirit. Do not be amazed that I said to you, 'You must be born again.'" (John 3:3–7)

You must be born again. That is, if you intend to get to heaven being a Pharisee, being a teacher, being a good man, being righteous, going through all the purification rites, well, unless you are born again, you are going to miss it.

There are lots of people who have done lots of things in order to prepare themselves to go to heaven. The only problem is they haven't done the one thing that will get them there, and they're going to be eternally disappointed. There is only one door, and that door is the person of Jesus Christ—and the way a person gets to heaven is by the experience we know as "the new birth."

The new birth is a *spiritual* experience, and a person may have many events in his or her life that lead up to it.

The new birth is a spiritual experience, and a person may have many events in his life that lead up to it. It may cover a period of time, but the experience itself is an instantaneous, momentary experience when, at that given moment, a person recognizes his sinfulness and acknowledges that Jesus Christ died on the cross for his sin and paid his sin debt in full. He confesses and repents of his sin and acknowledge his need of Christ, and his dependence upon Him for the forgiveness of his sin. Then he receives Jesus Christ by faith as his personal Savior for the forgiveness of his sins and commits himself to the person of Jesus Christ, recognizing that Jesus

Christ is none other than God Himself. That is what is called the new-birth experience.

Paul would have used this terminology. He said, "Therefore, if anyone is in Christ, he is a new creation" (2 Corinthians 5:17 ESV). The truth is that the new-birth experience is exactly what God says it is. It is a new beginning. It is a new birth. So for that person who is born again, not only is there a forgiveness of sin and a wiping away of guilt, but there is the coming of the Holy Spirit into that person's life to give him or her a new spirit.

Promises of a New Life in Heaven

He will swallow up death forever. The Sovereign Lord will wipe
away the tears from all faces; he will remove his people's disgrace
from all the earth. The Lord has spoken. In that day, they will say,
"Surely this is our God; we trusted in him, and he saved us. This is the
Lord, we trusted in him; let us rejoice and be glad in his salvation."
Isaiah 25:8–9 NIV

Since, then, you have been raised with Christ, set your hearts on
things above, where Christ is, seated at the right hand of God. Set
your minds on things above, not on earthly things. For you died,
and your life is now hidden with Christ in God. When Christ, who
is your life, appears, then you also will appear with him in glory.
Colossians 3:1–4 NIV

Yes, we are of good courage, and we would rather be
away from the body and at home with the Lord.
2 Corinthians 5:8 ESV

9

Becoming Eternally Secure

The miracle of the Holy Spirit is essential to the new-birth process. The new birth is not possible without God the Holy Spirit. When a person accepts Christ, when she allows Him into her heart and recognizes Him as her Savior, she is born again and cannot ever be what she was before because she has been born into a new life. Now she has a new spirit—a new life—and that life is the Lord Jesus Christ; that spirit is the Holy Spirit abiding and dwelling within her.

What makes us born again is the indwelling presence of the Holy Spirit. The Bible says all of us who are saved have been baptized by one Spirit into Christ Jesus. It is the presence of the Holy Spirit abiding and dwelling in you that makes you a child of God born again, or sealed, the Bible says, for the day of redemption (Ephesians 4:30).

It is the presence of the

Holy Spirit *abiding*

and dwelling in you that

makes you a child of God.

We might talk to God with our lips, but it is through our *spirits* with His Spirit that you and I relate to Him.

God gives the gift of His Spirit to those who are willing to receive Him. So, first of all, there has to be a transformation of character. In other words, how in the world could we ever have any relationship at all with a God when we are dead to Him and cannot communicate with Him? No, we have to embrace Him. We have to let Him into our hearts, to give Him that space inside us.

A New Spirit

Secondly, because God wants to develop a relationship with us, there must be a change—and that change is a transformation of a person's spirit where we are indwelt by the Holy Spirit, and we can communicate with God on the spirit level. Now, we might talk to Him with our lips, but it is through our spirits with His Spirit that you and I relate to Him.

Who is it that places that hunger and thirst and *yearning* in our hearts for God? Christ, living on the inside, places that hunger there.

You cannot bypass the Lord Jesus Christ. He knows the character of man. He knows our ultimate destination. He also knows what it takes to communicate with us and what it takes to develop a relationship with us, and He knows that means a total transformation of character. That is, a newness of life, the giving of a new spirit, becoming a new creation in Christ Jesus, and becoming something we've never been. And remember, He said He predestined you and me to be conformed to the likeness of His Son (Romans 8:29).

Do you think you could ever grow into the likeness of Jesus Christ apart from having a new spirit, a new desire? Who is it that places that hunger and thirst and yearning in our hearts for God? Christ, living on the inside, places that hunger there.

Jesus says that narrow is the gate that leads to heaven. There are few who find it (Matthew 17:13–14). And who are they? Those who drop their pride, their arrogance, their selfishness, and their self-righteousness and acknowledge they are destitute before God and unable to do anything about their sin problem. They acknowledge that Jesus Christ's death on the cross paid for their sins in full and in confession and repentance receive Him as personal Savior. That is the only hope you will ever have of getting to heaven, and there's not a single verse in all of God's Bible from Genesis to Revelation that even implies that you can get to heaven apart from a saving faith in Jesus Christ.

When you and I trust
the Lord Jesus Christ as
our *Savior*, we have
a divine nature, which
is an eternal nature.

An Experience Like the Wind

Now, with all that in mind, it's interesting what Jesus said to Nicodemus: "Do not marvel that I said to you, 'You must be born again.'" (John 3:7 NKJV).

Then they got into a discussion about how this experience is like the wind. You can't tell where it's coming from or where it's going. That is, you can't really see the new birth. You can see the results of it. It is a new life—a whole new perspective.

Jesus Christ comes into our lives through the Holy Spirit—that's the new-birth experience—so that you and I may live godly and holy before the Lord. And to believe in Jesus Christ is not merely to give intellectual assent to Him as a person, but to acknowledge in our spirits that He is God, and to confess and repent of our sins to Him. And we choose to follow Him as our Savior and our Lord.

When you and I trust the Lord Jesus Christ as our Savior, we have a divine nature, which is an eternal nature. It can never be separated from God. This simply means we have now become the

living sons and daughters of God. We are God's children and are eternally secure. Listen to what the apostle John said: "These things I have written to you who believe in the name of the Son of God, so that you may know that you have eternal life" (1 John 5:13).

Jesus put that in a very picturesque way when He said, "I am the way, the truth, and the life. I am the bread of life. I am the water of life. I am the light of life. I am the good shepherd. I am the door" (John 14:6; 6:35; 4:14; 8:12; 10:10, 7, paraphrased).

Jesus was saying, "If you want to get to heaven, this is it. You must accept Me personally." This is a really beautiful promise in its simplicity. By accepting Jesus into our hearts, we switch on a light inside us that transforms us. It allows for us to ascend into heaven. It allows for us to bloom into an unimaginable and eternal version of ourselves with a lasting and fulfilling connection to Jesus and to everyone around us. Jesus wants us all to enter into this relationship with Him. He wants us all to come to Him in heaven. He tells us that He is the first step, and the only way. He tells us that He is the door. All we have to do is walk through it and into the eternal and sacred bliss that is the kingdom of heaven.

Promises of the Narrow Way

I have been crucified with Christ. It is no longer I who live, but Christ who lives in me. And the life I now live in the flesh I live by faith in the Son of God, who loved me and gave himself for me.

Galatians 2:20 ESV

In this the love of God was made manifest among us, that God sent his only Son into the world, so that we might live through him. In this is love, not that we have loved God but that he loved us and sent his Son to be the propitiation for our sins. Beloved, if God so loved us, we also ought to love one another.

1 John 4:9–11 ESV

Give thanks to the God of heaven, for his steadfast love endures forever.

Psalm 136:26 ESV

10

The Best Is Yet to Come

*H*eaven is about God's love. For everything that we have covered in this book, it is just that simple. Heaven is about forever living in fellowship with God. It is the simplest and most complicated thing in the world. It is a gift, and it is a relationship. It is a narrow way. It is a beautiful and glorious promise of eternal life. It is a concept that is impossible to grasp, but beautiful and inspiring inside of that impossibility.

Heaven

is about

God's love.

We cannot fathom heaven. We cannot begin to even imagine its beauty. Instead, God traces the outlines of it for us. He provides a blueprint through His Word. We are God's children, and heaven is our home. So before this book comes to an end, I just want to reiterate the four essential things that God told us about this place that He has gone to prepare especially for us.

God is going to prepare a place for us. (JOHN 14:3)

First, heaven is not an imaginary place, an idea, or a celestial dream that you and I will experience forever and ever and ever. Jesus said, "I'm going to prepare a place." That is, a place where a glorified, literal body is going to communicate with other people and walk around and be somebody, and where we're going to know each other. God, the ultimate Creator, is making this heaven for us.

Our citizenship is in this place. (Philippians 3:20)

Second, God said our citizenship is in heaven. He also said in Luke 10 that our names have been written in heaven, in the Lamb's book of life (v. 20; also Revelation 21:27). So, if we have received Christ's gift of salvation, our citizenship is in this place and our names are recorded there, which means we will be there one of these days.

Our treasures are in heaven. (MATTHEW 6:20)

Third, Jesus said that we must lay up treasures, not on earth, but in heaven (Matthew 6:19–20). He was referring to all we give to God: our talents, our abilities, our time, and our service. These same gifts are the ones that will mark us in the renovated earth and New Jerusalem.

Our eternal home is still being created. (REVELATION 21:1–2)

Heaven is in two spheres, which leads me to believe that it's not complete yet. Notice the way Revelation 21 begins: "Then I saw a new heaven and a new earth; for the first heaven and the first earth passed away, and there is no longer any sea. And I saw the holy city, new Jerusalem, coming down out of heaven from God, made ready as a bride adorned for her husband."

In order for there to be a new earth, God is going to have to cleanse this earth of ours. When He comes back, He's going to wipe this earth absolutely clean and remake it. The heavens outside of it are going to be brand-new too. This is going to be done by the touch of holy God. It is going to be perfectly suited for us in our glorified bodies, which will not be limited by time, space, or substance.

This is our eternal home. This is our heaven.

With all this in mind, take a moment to join me in a prayer of thanks and praise to the God of heaven—our Father, the One who makes a place for us:

Dear God,

Thank You for loving us enough to prepare heaven for us. Thank You for giving us Your only Son as a door into this heavenly home, this place where You have allowed us to belong. You have created the sun, the moon, the stars, and worlds beyond ours that are unimaginable and brilliant. You continue to create and invent ways to bring Your everlasting light to us. You have prepared us for heaven by giving us glimpses of the wonder and grace, the community and the fellowship, that will exist in heaven. We are excited to live forever inside our relationship with You. We want that oneness and that closeness and that fulfillment and that love. Please guide us on earth now, so that we may live eternally by Your side. Thank You for this miracle. Thank You, God, for our heavenly home, amen.

$\mathcal{D}$r. Charles Stanley is the senior pastor of First Baptist Church of Atlanta, Georgia, where he has served for more than forty years. He is a *New York Times* bestselling author who has written more than sixty books, including the top devotional *Every Day in His Presence*. Dr. Stanley is the founder of In Touch Ministries. The *In Touch with Dr. Charles Stanley* program is transmitted throughout the world on more than 1,200 radio outlets, 130 television stations/networks, and in language projects in more than 50 languages. The award-winning *In Touch* devotional magazine is printed in four languages, with more than 12 million copies each year. Dr. Stanley's goal is best represented by Acts 20:24, "Life is worth nothing unless I use it for doing the work assigned me by the Lord Jesus—the work of telling others the Good News about God's mighty kindness and love" (TLB). This is because, as he says, "It is the Word of God and the work of God that changes people's lives."